# Dog T

MW01290018

# *The Definitive Step by Step Guide to The Most Loving, Obedient, Happy & Well-Trained Dog!*

© **Copyright 2016**

All rights Reserved. No part of this book may be reproduced in any form without permission in writing from the author. Reviewers may quote brief passages in reviews.


**Disclaimer**

No part of this publication may be reproduced or transmitted in any form or by any means, mechanical or electronic, including photocopying or recording, or by any information storage and retrieval system, or transmitted by email without permission in writing from the publisher.

While all attempts have been made to verify the information provided in this publication, neither the author nor the publisher assumes any responsibility for errors, omissions or contrary interpretations of the subject matter herein.

This book is for entertainment purposes only. The views expressed are those of the author alone, and should not be taken as expert instruction or commands. The reader is responsible for his or her own actions.

Adherence to all applicable laws and regulations, including international, federal, state and local laws governing professional licensing, business practices, advertising and all other aspects of doing business in the US, Canada, UK or any other jurisdiction is the sole responsibility of the purchaser or reader.

Neither the author nor the publisher assumes any responsibility or liability whatsoever on the behalf of the purchaser or reader of these materials. Any perceived slight of any individual or organization is purely unintentional.

# Table of Contents

# Introduction

If you have purchased this book, the odds are you either have a very disobedient member of your family who needs some training or you have recently brought a new family member into your household. Either way you might be feeling a little overwhelmed and looking for information that can help you handle whatever may be happening with your four legged friend.

In this book I will talk about different training tactics to help you gain control over your pack. You can say I take a bit of a "Caesar" approach to dog training but it works and I for one do not like disciplining my animals the way some people feel they must. But to each there own, in this book though we will discuss different tactics that mimic how a real leader would keep his pack in line.

We will go over things like crate training, potty training, general commands as well as some tips and tricks that will help you with your training. I want to help you with a step by step guide to training your dog in all the basics. This will give you and your pup a good base to move forward from with any other training you may want to do.

One of the most important concepts of this book is that you create a bond with your dog or dogs and you become their leader. You need to find that line between being their companion and the own who keeps them in line. By praising them for good behavior and correcting the wrong behavior in a manner similar to the alpha dog your bond will grow. People sometimes forget that dogs aren't people and though we have domesticated them for 1000s of years they still don't understand us like we would hope they do.

We will talk about body language and asserting your confidence. You need to be assertive, you need to know that you are in charge of your pack and they relay that to your dogs. If they sense weakness they will take advantage of it. There will also be times where they will probably test you and you will need to correct them. But when you can step up and be their leader your dogs will be so much happier for it. They will know where their place is in the pack and not feeling like they need to lead, this comfort of know where their place is will create a calmer, happier and more well adjusted dog.

Hopefully by the end of this book you will be a more confident and more prepared dog owner. I can't promise that you will be an expert, but I can certainly give you the tools you need to become your pack leader. Hopefully the confidence to train your dogs and help them become the happy well adjusted animals they want to be. No dog wants to be aggressive or do things that upset their pack leader and with the tools I will give you in this book you will be able to give your dogs what they need to become that animal you always hoped they would be.

# Chapter 1: Becoming The Pack Leader

If you read none of the other chapters in this book this one will serve you the best. The most important part to working with your dog is becoming their leader. Dogs in the wild live in packs and those packs have a hierarchy, with the alpha at the top, in order for your dog or dogs to become the happy well adjusted animals you want you need to be the leader of your pack. That way your dogs can follow your example and they wont need to feel stressed thinking that they need to be the leader.

One common mistake many owners make when they are having issues with aggression or their dog misbehaving or defying them is thinking that the dog is showing true aggression, or that they are simply defying them. For almost all dogs the problem lies in their owner, the one in their lives that is supposed to be their leader, doesn't lead them. If you don't give your dog the discipline they need and the leadership they crave to know their position in their world, then they will be lost. They don't understand the way we function in a family and they will try to fill the gap they believe is there by thinking they need to be the pack leader. This is where we see this undesirable behavior. It is a manifestation of their fear and insecurity with their place and the order in their life. So when you can take that perceived gap and become your dogs pack leader you will see a happier animal.

Hopefully I have been able to impress upon you how important it is to become the pack leader. So now that I have been telling you how important it is for your animal to have someone to follow let's talk about how your going to get there. There are a few things you can work on that will help your dog to see you as the leader and they are fairly simple things in concept but are harder to execute and for some people will take a fair amount of work to accomplish.

**Find Your Confidence:** The first step to success is finding your confidence. The key for anyone being a leader is confidence. You have to believe that you can do this. You have to find the fortitude in yourself and allow your confidence to grow. If you can't find your confidence in yourself, you wont be able to inspire your dogs to follow you so this is key.

**Believe You Are the Leader:** Once you have started to find your confidence, in yourself and your abilities you then need to believe that you are the leader of this pack. You need to believe that you can do this because if you do not believe none of the animals you hope to lead will. Being their leader is a simple thing, your dogs don't require much from their alpha so don't think you have to dictate everything in their lives if you become their alpha. Just like being a parent and needing to correct and guide your child it is a similar path for your animals. You don't need to dictate their every movement or choice. The idea is to guide them to the right choice and teach them what is acceptable and unacceptable. When you look at being the pack leader from this prospective it may make it easier to believe that not only can you lead but that you are capable of giving your dogs the guidance they need.

**Exude That Confidence in Your Actions:** The final step is to take the confidence and that belief that you are the pack leader and exude it in all of your actions with your animals. An alpha dog has a calm quiet demeanor, where as a dog not meant to be a leader will be loud, all bark no bite. The alpha is not afraid to discipline when another dog steps out of line. You need to be the same way, allow your dogs freedom when but when they step out of line you need to figure out a sound or action that lets your pack know you are unhappy with those actions. You need to be calm and confident when you walk your dog, when you ask anything of your animal. That quiet confidence will give you what you need to make your dogs understand exactly what you want and that you are their pack leader.

So you might be saying to yourself at this point, yea easier said then done with this confidence stuff and your totally right. Telling you to find your confidence is the easy part, having you find it can be the difficult part. Some people take to this like a fish to water and they just have that confidence and with a little guidance its just there. For others it's not so easy. But don't fear I am going to go over some exercises you can do to help you harness any other feelings you may be having besides quiet confidence.

**Start with Breathing:** Let's first start with some breathing exercises to help you calm down and control any fears or nervousness you may be feeling when you start thinking about training your dog. Your dog does not need to be around at first, I just want you to sit somewhere comfortable and while thinking about training your dog I want you to take slow deep breaths and access how your body is feeling. Is there tension or nervousness in any area of your body? If there is, I want you to work on relaxing it while continuing to breath slowly. For some this will be extremely easy to master, if so move on to doing the same activity with your dog in the room and then finally while your dog in on the leash. It's okay if you don't fly through this part, relaxing and finding your calm, quiet, confidence will be harder for some and that's perfectly fine. Remember everyone is different and will move at their own pace.

**Mental Picture:** Another tactic that can help build your confidence is picturing your success in your mind. If you can imagine you looking cool and confident while walking your pet, you can have an image to hold on and help you aspire to. Picturing your goal before attempting it can help keep you on track.

**Find Your Sound:** The last thing I want you to do is find your sound. I am sure you have seen other dog trainers or owners give a certain noise that lets their dogs know they are displeased with whatever behavior they are exhibiting. I want you to find out what sound works for you so you can use it whenever you find you need to correct any furry friend in your home. When they understand that particular sound means they did something wrong they will start to understand certain actions gains that sound and through that sound the displeasure of the pack leader which will in turn stop the behavior. It should be a quick, sharp sound that will get your dogs attention but nothing too loud as you need to be a quiet and calm pack leader to inspire confidence in your dogs to follow you.

**The "Bite":** With your sound you can also administer a "bite". To put it more simply this is meant to be a quick and decisive touch that will redirect your animal's attention and let them know you are unhappy with a certain behavior. It is meant to mimic a bite the pack leader would give to a member who wasn't listening or were exhibiting behaviors that were attempting to assert dominance. Please note that the "bite" is not supposed to hurt your animal in anyway it truly is a touch just meant to mimic that sort of correction a pack leader would give. I don't want you to think you really need to bite your dog or anything crazy. But you do need to mimic what another dog would do in that situation to really get through to your pup. This concept can be really hard for people to understand because you think of your dog as your buddy or family member and many forget that at the end of the day they are animals. They aren't going to understand people and other animals like they can understand the signals given by other dogs.

All these tools are meant to help you find your confidence and become the best pack leader you can be. By fulfilling that role your dog so desperately needs you to, everyone will be on their way to a happier and calmer home. Remember no matter how much you love your dog they are still a dog and need boundaries and guidance.

Even with all this advice you will still need to tailor this to your needs. Everyone is different and you will need to find how being the leader works for you and your family. But you still need to be that leader, you need to be the top dog so that your furry friend knows where his or her place is in the pack. If you aren't the leader, then no one in your house will be happy or well adjusted.

# Chapter 2: Potty Training

One of the most common dog training problems is potty training. Some dogs can have an especially difficult time grasping the concept of going to the bathroom outside and for puppy parents of these hard learners' life can become especially frustrating. I am going to give you a very simple system that will work for puppies or even slightly older dogs that are ready to potty train or could use some better training. Whatever age your dog is and whatever level of training they have you should be able to implement this system to help you both achieve an acceptable level of training for their age.

First of all, I really need you to try and keep your emotions under control when you go to train your puppy. Yes, the process can be frustrating and sometimes your furry friend is going to try your patience but there are some very serious reasons why you don't want your buddy to see your frustration. I have helped train some difficult animals but one of the more difficult and common problems I run into animals who become fearful of going in front of their owners. What we as doggie parents don't realize is that our furry friends can misunderstand our anger with accidents thinking it is the fact that they are going to the bathroom instead of associating it with going in the house. This creates a fear in your dogs about going when you can see them. Many pet owners don't have a yard they can just let their dog out in and have to put them on a leash or take them for a walk so they can go to the bathroom. If you create this fear in them, you will have a hard time potty training particularly if they need to be on a leash to go to the bathroom. This is just one example of the type of problem you can run into if you can't keep your emotions in check while your potty training. So with this said try to keep your frustration and other feelings to a minimum as you are potty training your dog.

**Step 1:** The first step to training seems like the most basic one but it works and is the most important to establishing good guide lines for your dog. Take your dog out and often. If its a puppy, they need to pee more often then you will probably realize. If you have ever had children, then you will have an idea of how often a puppy needs to go at first. They only have a little bladder so try to take your dog out every hour. Even if they are older, try to take them out every hour that you are home.

**Step 2:** Praise! When you have your dog outside and they do go to the bathroom you need to praise them. Make a fuss, get them excited. If they are excited for your reaction they will be excited about going to the bathroom and doing something that pleases you. It is very rare to encounter a dog who is not a people please especially when that dog sees you as the pack leader.

**Step 3:** Fixing the mistakes as they come is the next important step to potty training. If your furry friend has an accident in the house you need to keep your cool. Take them immediately outside, especially if you catch them in the act. I know your natural instinct is to yell but try your hardest not to. You do not want them scared to go to the bathroom in front of you. Otherwise you could wind up with the hider and find surprises all over your house because your pup is hiding from you as they do their business. I know this part can be frustrating but if you keep up with it long enough they will realize that you want them going to the bathroom outside.

**Step 4:** As your pup gets more used to going to the bathroom outside you can cut back how often they go out as they build up their bladder muscles. Try to never make your dog hold their bladder longer then 10 to 12 hours. Once they are full sized and they have learned to hold themselves you will be able to leave them home alone longer. But anything longer then that amount of time and you risk them getting an infection or hurting themselves, if they can even hold it. So slowly cut back how often you let them out starting with every 2 hours then every 3 hours and so on and so on. Do it slowly and make sure you pay attention to your furry buddy. If you see signs that they need to go to the bathroom like excessive sniffing or circling, then you should take them right out. Your better off taking longer to stretch out the time between going to the bathroom then letting them accidentally go in the house. You don't want them to associate in anyway that its easier or at all okay to go to the bathroom in the house. You will make your life that much harder if you don't. But once your pup has learned to hold their bladder and gained control over their muscles, and they don't have any medical issues, there is no reason they shouldn't be able to hold themselves for 6 to 8 hours while you are at work.

The steps for potty training in and of themselves are very simple. But they are most certainly effective in teaching your pup to go outside. You have to remember that there is no easy fix for potty training your dog. I wish I could give you a method where it would require no work on your part and that all dogs could be trained. It would be wonderful but like just about everything else in life you need to work for what you want. So try to keep a positive outlook while you are potty training and remember that this is only temporary. When you put the hard work in early you will set your dog up for success and save yourself a lot of trouble later on. Potty training a puppy is really a simple process it just takes some dedication and consistency to have an amazingly trained dog that you can leave home alone for some time without worrying if they will go to the bathroom in the house.

# Chapter 3: Crate Training

While our furry friends are amazing parts of our family and we love and trust them in so many ways it can also make many nervous to leave them alone to roam the house when we are not home. Some dogs can get anxiety when their owners are away and we see that manifest in destructive behaviors like chewing and going to the bathroom in the house. These same behaviors can be exhibited when your animals are bored or even scared at being home alone. There are lots of different feelings that can incite these destructive behaviors in your animals when you're not around so its totally understandable for owners to feel a little leery about leaving their furry buddies on their own when they aren't around.

Thankfully their is a solution if your dog has issues with these types of feelings when you are not around. You can crate train them, giving them a safe space that is all their own. When done properly your dog will sleep or just go into their crate to hang out even when they don't need to. Then when you're not home, being in the crate will help with many of those feelings because they will be in their safe space. They will be perfectly comfortable in their crate while you are gone and you as a pet owner wont have to worry about accidents all over the house and your things getting destroyed. Here are some benefits to crate training:

-They will house train faster. Puppies and dogs that learn to crate train will typically potty train faster because they have too. When they are in their crate for periods of time they have to learn to hold it so they wind up laying in it.

-It gives you dog a space where they feel secure. When your dog knows they have a safe place where they can relax or sleep they will be happier. Dogs have a natural instinct to find a "den" so by giving them a crate you can fulfill that instinct.

-This can keep your puppy safe while you can't watch them. Puppies are just like babies in a sense that they don't know what will hurt them and what wont yet. Just like with kids they need to learn as they need to learn what they can chew on and what they cannot chew on. The crate keeps them safe from dangers in your house and your house safe from your puppy.

-Sometimes you are going to want to go on trips or you may even have to move for work. Whatever your circumstances are you will need to transport your furry friend in some way at some point. Even if its just a trip to the vet. By helping them learn the crate is there safe space you wind up with a safe way to transport them if you ever need to.

-Puppies can be a handful at times and they can get very hyper just like children. Sometimes you may not be able to get them to calm down simple by working with them. The crate is a great way to put them in a quite place so they can safely calm down. It is a tool that can help you manage certain behaviors as long as you use it properly.

-Boarding at the vet's or a kennel. Unfortunately, almost every dog winds up spending some times in a crate weather you have to board them when you go on vacation or they need to be crated to recover after a medical treatment. By getting your pup used to it early they will have time to adjust instead of having to force the issue because you need it.

The most critical part of getting a crate is getting something that fits your dog. If you get a crate that is too big and they have a lot of freedom to move, they will not attempt to hold themselves because they don't have too. When they can get away from the mess and don't have to lay in it they won't hold it. I know it sounds mean to put your pup in a crate and only give them about enough room to turn around, stand up and lay down comfortably in but not only will it prevent messes but they will also feel more secure. If you are getting a puppy, you don't have to buy different crates to fit them as they go. Do a little research figure out about how big they will be and buy a single crate that will accommodate that size. The nice thing about crates now is you can buy ones with inserts that allow you to adjust the amount of room available to your pup. So as they grow you can expand the area they have to accommodate their size. I really need to stress this if you are going to crate train, if you plan on leaving your pup alone for a few hours while you go out and do anything, work, grocery shop, whatever it may be they need to fit in their crate and be comfortable in order for it to work properly.

There are times when you should never crate your dog because they can do harm to themselves. No matter how much you may not trust them or worry they will damage your house these signs should be addressed and not ignored. These are the signs of separation anxiety, fear of the crate or potentially claustrophobia.

-If there is damage to the crate that shows signs of attempting to escape. It is one thing if your pup is bored or angry with your for leaving or whatever the case may be and chew on something in the crate. But if the signs point to they attempting to get out then they don't feel safe in their crate and instead see it as cage which can cause major anxiety.

-Signs that they are salivating excessively. When anxiety levels go up they will pant to try and cool and calm themselves. So if you find dampness on their bodies or inside the crates the odds are it's from salivating and you should monitor them while they spend time in their crate.

-Relieving themselves while in the crate. Though it may be that they simply couldn't hold it until you got home or you could have the crate to large and because they are able to get away from the mess they don't see any reason to hold themselves. If you find they are going in the crate often you should begin to monitor them and make sure they aren't going to the bathroom out of fear and that it is instead one of these other issues.

-Damage to things outside of the crate. If you come home and find that anything within reach has been damaged by your pup while they were safely locked inside, then you will probably need to consider another method as this is another sign of their anxiety once in the crate.

-The crate has moved. Sometimes while your dog is inside the crate they will have so much movement that it can actually move the crate across the floor. There movements inside the crate have to be fairly frantic to move the large object across the floor. If you notice this, you will want to monitor your dog while inside the crate to make sure they aren't thrashing about you don't want them to hurt themselves.

For the most part many dogs are perfectly happy and comfortable in their crates. But there are a few that will have too much anxiety to be able to affectively use the crate. If this is the case, you will have to find an alternative or get some help training them to get over their fears because if you don't the odds are they will hurt themselves.

There are some things you should never use the crate for. Yes, it is a useful tool but there are certain times when it may be tempting to use their crate and you will wind up creating more problems for yourself.

-You should never have your dog crated for longer then they can hold their bladder. If you push them too long to hold it can create a whole host of issues. They can get a bladder infection from having the bacteria in their too long. They can obviously go to the bathroom in their crate but this can lead to resentment of the crate because they were in pain in there or they can start to think its perfectly acceptable to go in there. Don't make things worse for yourself do your best to make sure they are never in their longer then they can hold themselves.

-If your dog is sick or fighting with diarrhea you do not want to put them in the crate. They are already not feeling good and locking them in to live in the mess you know they are going to create is just mean because they will continue to get sick and then they won't be able to get away from it. They also will most likely not have access to fresh water which can quickly dehydrate a sick dog. Instead corral them to a certain area of the house and make sure they have plenty of water available.

-When the weather gets extremely hot you should never have your pup in a crate. It's one thing if they are in a nice conditioned house but when it's very hot and they can't get somewhere that's cooler you risk them overheating. You also run the same risk of them dehydrating as most crates have no way to include fresh water for them.

-You should never have your furry friend in their crate for anymore then 5 to 8 hours. 5 is the recommended maximum amount of time to keep from having bladder issues. But if they are healthy and well trained they should be able to hold themselves for about 8 hours if you really need them too.

-If for any reason your vet has specifically prohibited crating your dog then you need to follow their instructions. You can get creative with how you will confine them to one area if they are the type of destroy things when your gone but you still need to follow your vet's instructions to give your dog the best care.

-You should never use the crate to punish your animal. You do not want them to have negative feelings associated with their crate. If you use it for punishment it will no longer be the safe place where they can hide away and feel secure. It will literally become a punishment for them no matter what you may be using it for at that moment and it will create a bigger problem.

-I know our pets can be trying at times and can even cause frustration but under no circumstances should your put them in the crate just to get them out of the way or because you just don't feel like dealing with them. That is not what this tool was meant for and it's not fair to your furry friend.

-If your pet is crated for more then half of its time then you might want to consider rehoming them or making more of an effort to spend time with them. Dogs are not meant to be cooped up in this manor and its cruel. We all understand life happens and you have to work, and some pups need to sleep in the crate at night. But if you pay attention to your schedule and realize they are almost always in their crate then it's time to make a change because it is unhealthy for your furry friend.

Now that we have talked about some do's and don'ts with your crate as well as the importance of choosing the proper size lets move on to making your pup's crate a safe and comfortable place for them to be. You want them to love spending time in there, if they enjoy it in there it will make your life that much easier.

-Keep the crate in a room where you spend a lot of time. This will help them associate the crate with good things and will help keep them from feeling isolated or rejected.

-You want the crate to be out of direct sunlight as well as away from any heat sources or particularly cold spots in the house. This keeps them from getting too hot or too cold with the inability to get away if they are uncomfortable.

-Put soft bedding in the crate for your pup to lay on. If they are a puppy, you should try to find bedding that is difficult for them to chew so they can't destroy it. This will keep them comfortable and cozy in their space.

-Keep at least two chew toys inside their crate to keep them occupied while they are in there. Not only does this promote good chew toy habits but it will keep your buddy from getting bored.

-If you have a wire crate for your dog you should cover it with either a blanket or a crate cover. This will help promote that enclosed den like feel that your dog will love. If you are using something other than a fitted crate cover just monitor your dog that they don't pull your cover through and destroy it.

-Last but by far the most important factor to remember when using the crate is your dog should have their leash removed before going into their crate. I recommend you remove their collar as well but the key to this is that you don't want your pup to be able to get tangled or caught. Either outcome they could get seriously injured or die if they get chocked somehow. Crates are meant to be a safe place for your friend to hang out when you can't keep an eye on them so make sure that they are safe in there or you will never forgive yourself for accidentally hurting them.

## Crate Training

**Step 1**-Convincing your dog that the crate is a positive thing.

This first step is easy and can be kind of fun but it is very important to accomplish and if you can you will make your life that much easier on the next steps to training. There are a few things you can do to help convince your dog that the crate is a magical and amazing place to be.

Start by assembling your crate either before your puppy comes home or if you already have your dog assemble it when they aren't around so that it just seems to appear one day. When you first introduce the crate you actually want to ignore its presence, pretend it isn't even there if you can and don't praise or say anything when your dog goes into it. You want them to think there is nothing unusual about it and have them simply accept it like its no big deal which they will de by follow your example. You are the pack leader and if something isn't a big deal to you the odds are your dogs will follow your example.

Have treats and toys magically appear in the crate. When they see it for the first time you want to sprinkle some treats in front of the crate as well as some at the front of the crate and a few more at the back. You can also put some of their favorite toys or new toys inside as well. The whole idea with this part is to get them into the mindset that the crate is super cool and has great things appear around it. Make sure they don't see you put the treats or toys in the crate as that will take the mystery away from the crate for them. They are naturally curious and they will assume that the crate make the delicious things appear making them like it all the more.

Do this for a few days just letting them get used to the crate. When they leave the room you can sprinkle some more treats or replace the toys inside the crate so that whenever they come back into the room the crate has magically created more good things. This strong association with good things will help your dog learn to love the crate. The next step is to start feeding your dog in the crate. After a few days of magical treats and toys start feeding with the food bowl just inside the crate so all they have to do is stick their head inside. Depending on how fearful of the crate they are you may need to do this for a few days to a week before your able to move the food bowl to the back of the crate.

Once they have the idea they will literally run into their crate whenever they see you coming with the food bowl. Most dogs love to eat and giving them a secure and cozy place to eat their food will make them love the crate that much more.

**Step 2**- Picking your commands and teaching your pup them.

You should pick two different commands, one that let's your dog know when you would like them to get in the crate and one that let's them know that it's okay to leave the crate. Most people are very consistent with the first one but they forget to teach the dog when its okay to leave the crate. If you forget this step you will run into to problems when you want to do things like give them an extra toy but don't want them to leave the crate, or they will bolt out potentially bowling you over, or you sometimes will have to deal with them not wanting to get out of the crate when you need them too and you wind up dragging them out. None of these are necessarily fun outcomes to opening the crate door so if you make it a command then you wont have to fight with your pup which makes life easier in the long run. During the next few exercises I would like you to either take the door off of or secure it so that it can't accidentally close on your dog and upset them or scare them.

So choose your commands and use them consistently through out training to have them go in and out of their crate. You can say something like "crate up" or "kennel up" it can even be something silly like "okay girlfriend" or "in you get buddy". Whatever you like as long as you say them consistently so they know what you are asking.

To teach your dog these commands you are now going to start asking them to enter the crate. Entice them with treats and as they complete the desired action you will say the command you have chosen to they start to associate the command with the action and of coarse good things because almost all dogs love food. The first time just toss the treat in letting them go in on their own without much more encouragement, then once they do make a big fuss giving them another treat while inside their crate. Next move quietly and slowly away from the crate so they can exit on their own and once they do without encouragement from you give them lots of praise. Don't give them a treat for exiting the crate as you want them to only associate that with going into the crate, remember the whole idea here is to make them love their crate and think its the most awesome place in the world. Make sure you are saying those cue words as they start to complete the action, saying it every time over and over again will help them understand. Do this about 8 to 10 times then give your furry friend a break. Repeat this exercise quite a few times over the next day or two until they are really confident with going in the crate to get their treat.

**Step 3**-Make them work for those treats.

Now that you have your dog's confidence up I want you to ask them into the crate before you give them the treat. If you have been consistently using your cue words you dog shouldn't have any trouble understanding what your asking. Start the first time or two with throwing the treat in and then once they have gone in and out a few times like normal then give the cue without throwing the treat. Hopefully they will hop in the crate without thinking. Once they do give them lots of praise while giving them a treat or two. Then continue your exercise as normal letting them exit and asking them to go back but wait to give the treat for the rest of the session. Repeat this the first time or two as your pup transitions before moving on to asking first every time. Repeat asking them in before giving the treat throughout the day for a day or two until they are just as confident as they were with following the treat in. Make sure they really understand what your asking with those cues and that they are happy to go in and out of the crate.

If you go to move onto this step and you find that your pup is nervous about going in or doesn't follow your cue, then you probably progressed too soon and go back to the first step until you feel that they are confident enough to move on.

**Step 4**-Sitting and lying down in the crate.

The next big step to training is getting them to sit and lay down when in the crate. When you first get your dog you should be using training them to sit, lay down and stay on cue. I will be going over this in a later chapter so feel free to move on to that chapter to help you with this next stage if you haven't already started.

The process is pretty much the same, give them the cue to go in the crate and give them their treat then acting like nothing has changed ask them to sit and give them big praise and another treat when they do. Then ask for them to lay down and again praise and give them a treat. Once they have done both then give the cue to leave the crate. Repeat this 8 to 10 times each time you do it and do the exercise through out the day. Also keep the amount of time that you ask them to stay varied you don't want them to get into the habit of it being the same amount of time. Dogs are smart and if you are too consistent they will just repeat the actions without actually being asked because they know that produces a treat. By keeping it varied you will keep their attention. You also want to start slowing stretching the times out asking them to eventually stay longer and longer. Continue practicing this for another day or two.

Remember to continue feeding your dog all his meals in the crate while your training them.

**Step 5**-Shutting the door.

Once they are used to and comfortable with the crate it's time to start shutting the door and the eventual goal is to be able to place them in the crate when needed. You will probably have been working on these exercises for about a week or so to have your pup ready for this point. Some dogs may be faster and some may be slower depending on their personality.

Start with repeating the exercises they are used to with the sit, lay down and stay. Then after completing that a few times you want to shut the door. Just do it nice and slow act like its no big deal and then feed them a few treats through the closed door to encourage that the calm behavior is a good thing. If they get panicky then try only shutting the door halfway for as many session as it takes for you dog to start to be calm with the door like that. You may need to progress slower but if you rush this part you will undo all the hard work you have done so don't push your pup.

When they are used to the door being close you can then start to latch it for a few seconds at a time. Keep this up repeating 8 to 10 repetitions at a time slowly working your dog up until they can sit calmly in the crate for a whole minute.

**Step 6**- Leaving them to their own devices.

The last step is to walk away. Once you have them used to everything and staying calm with the door latched you then want to start walking away as part of the routine. Keep it short at first and slowly progress until it is longer. It also helps if you stay in the room at first before you start exiting the room. It is always important to keep where you go and how long your away varied and never do more then 10 repetitions at a time or your dog will get bored.

After they are more used to this you can leave them in there for longer and longer periods of time. Sometimes when you feed them leave them in there with their food and their favorite toy for a while. Keep the first few times you leave the house short then slowly increase. Once they are more and more used to having some time to themselves in the crate and they are okay with you leaving the room and the house they will eventually be okay with the entire process. Remember to not make a fuss when you leave or some back from being outside. This will help to reinforce that this is no big deal and a normal part of being in the house. You are the pack leader and your dog will take his or her cues from you so as long as you act like it's no big deal it wont be one for them.

It may suck to have to corral them somewhere in the house when you have to leave for work if you are not able to stay home with your new addition for those few first days but it will be worth the effort when you have a happy well adjusted pup who loves his crate.

Try to have at least one or two special toys that they only get inside their crate like a stuffed Kong or whatever it is they really like. If they associate that they will only get that special toy once inside the crate they will look forward to their time in there because of their special treat.

Just remember to go at your dogs pace, some dogs can be crate trained in a weekend while others may take weeks. If you have gotten your dog from a rescue that had them in kennels often you may find them more resistive but no matter what the circumstance if you go slow and give them lots of encouragement you will be able to have a happy and confident pup who loves their crate. Crate training can go horribly wrong if not executed properly and doggie owners can be left with a very difficult dog who hates their crate. You can even create anxiety in your animals so I strongly recommend reading these steps well and following them as best you can. Once they develop a strong dislike for the crate it can be a very hard thing to turn around so I encourage you to try and train them right the first time and save yourself a lot of potential aggravation and fear on the part of your dog.

# Chapter 4: Basic Training (Sit, Stay, Come Etc.)

There are a couple of basic cues that are important for you dog to understand and if you take the time to teach them you will be happier for your effort. The ones I like to teach to dogs are Sit, Down, Stay, Come, Focus, Wait, and Free. The first four should be fairly recognizable and are all great to teach the last three aren't taught as often but they can be extremely helpful to having a well trained furry friend. Focus is used to get your dogs attention on your when their may be other distracting things going on around them. This is great if they are excited about another animal or person and you find they are ignoring your cues. If you start with focus first and get their attention on you they will then hopefully be focused well enough to complete the other commands. Wait is a cue I give typically when out for a walk, this is similar to heel as it teaches them that you essentially want them to come back to your side and essentially wait for you to move on or give the command that they can go. Free is the cue I use to release my pets from whatever activity they have been doing. My dogs are great but if you asking them to stay and forget about them they will stay for hours so I always like to teach this cue so you can say free and your dog is free to do as they please. I will go over how to train each of these simple commands and then it will be up to you to practice with your dogs and reinforce the training in their minds.

**Focus**- I teach this command first because it is actually fairly easy to do and once your dog has gotten the hang of it, it can be extremely useful in teaching all of the other tricks. Some dogs also get very excited about food and when they learn this one properly they will calm down and focus on you instead of jumping up and down for their snack.

Grab some treats and call your dog over to you. As they focus on you and the treat in your hand say your cue word and then give them the treat. Repeat a few times, say focus and as soon as your pup has zoned in on you and the treat repeat the word and then give a treat. Repeat this a few times but when training try to not do more then 10 times in a row without a break in between. You don't want your dog to get overwhelmed or bored, this rule will apply for training all of these cues.

Slowly extend the amount of time you get them to focus on you before giving the treat, eventually you will be able to give the command and no matter where they are they will look to you for direction recognizing you want their attention.

**Sit**- This is a pretty basic command and one almost every dog owner has given their dog at one time or another. Even the ones who haven't necessarily taught it to their animals still try to use it because it is so common and very useful.

Start with your focus and once your dog is focused in on your and the treat I want you to have the treat close to their nose but don't let them have it and then slowly move it towards the back of their tail while holding above their head. If they follow the treat properly the movement will cause them to involuntarily sit to keep the treat in view. As soon as they start to sit give the sit command and once they have sat give them a treat and praise. Repeat until they are confident. If they are resistive holding the treat above their head as you move it towards their tail you can take the other hand and press light on their back very close to their hips, this light pressure with the treat movement will help move more resistive dogs into the proper position.

Once they have this down and they are doing it confidently give the command without the hand movement and see if they sit. Make sure you do the usual command a few times first before doing this in the same set of repetitions. (A lot of the processes here are similar to the ones used for crate training so don't be afraid to refer back to that chapter for the process on repetitions) As long as you have given the voice command every time when they sit they will start to associate and you should be able to move into this next step. If not go back and reinforce before moving on until they can sit without moving your hand or the physical touch.

I know it sounds so simple but that's really all there is to it, that and being consistent. Work on it often giving lots of praise and treats when they do it right. Positive reinforcement is the best training for dogs and it also helps inspire their confidence in you as a leader especially if you can keep from yelling or getting angry with them.

**Down**- The next step is getting your dog to lay down. I like to use the command down it is fairly universal and if you can keep your cues something simple and to the point then anyone who may have to handle your pet will be able to give commands even if you can't be around.

Start with focus and then sit, once you have gone through the usual exercises a few times then ask your dog down. Take the treat, holding it in front of their nose and move it towards the floor as they follow and head towards the floor say your command word. They might not lay all the way down at first but that's okay praise them for heading in the right direction. Once they start to get the idea you can do a few things to get them to totally lay down if they aren't all ready. You can try holding the treat down their closed in their hand. They will most likely try to get it out but don't give it up as they get frustrated trying to reach it many will lay down because they don't want to hold themselves up any longer. That's when you'll repeat the command and give them the treat with praise. Others may require a gentle push down on the shoulder blades with one hand while holding the other on the floor by their nose. Make sure its gentle steady pressure and they will get the idea. When they give to the pressure repeat your command and give them the treat and praise. Use which ever method works best for your pup and repeat multiple times a day in short sessions until they are confident with it.

**Stay-** Once you have the basic commands down this is the next in the natural progression of things. This command can be a lot more difficult for many dogs especially once you get to the stage of turning away from them. Many dogs with be okay as long as they can see your face and are focused but when you break eye contact it will be harder for them to remain focused on their task so don't get frustrated if you reach this snag.

Start with the usual cues focus and sit. I recommend teaching them to stay while sitting first because it is a more comfortable position for many dogs then laying down typically is. They can feel more exposed when laying down so this can make the concept of stay harder then it needs to be. Once they have sat and are remaining in place then speak your command word and give them a treat. Do this a few times getting them used to the new command before moving on. Make sure they they remain in a seated position while giving the command. Though they will barely have to wait to be treated you don't want them jumping up while giving the command but if you have gained proper focus this shouldn't be an issue.

Next you will get your sit and then issue the stay command and keeping their focus you will have them hold the sit for a few seconds before giving them a treat and praise. This particular cue many dogs love because they think they are getting a treat for doing nothing which they technically are but we understand the value of teaching them to stay. Continue with these exercises varying the time and lengthening as you go. Once they seem pretty confident with this you will then start to move once you have issued the command keep your movements small and first and praise them immediately when they do not move even though you are. Keep this up making the movement more and more with bigger and bigger steps to the side or away from them. Make sure they stay until you come back to them to give them the treat and praise. This will reinforce that staying put will get you to come to them and give them the treat when they listen.

Eventually you will start turning your back after issuing the command. Keep it brief at first and eventually make it longer giving lots of praise with every success. If they fail at this point, getting up when they lose your eye contact just ignore the behavior and reset them. If they don't get any reaction or treat when they get up but get treats and praise when they stay they will soon realize what you are looking for. With practice you should be able to break eye contact and leave the room or outside area they are in and they shouldn't move until you tell them it's okay. Once you have it with sit you will then move on to getting them to stay while laying down. Try to not get frustrated if this takes some time, like I mentioned earlier dogs feel more vulnerable while laying down so it may take some time for them to be more comfortable staying in a laying position.

**Free**- I tend to teach free and stay at the same time. I focus more on gaining the stay but I will speak the free command often when working with my dog. Every time you treat them and they begin to move around of their own free will speak the word free. Eventually they will equate the freedom of movement with the word. I try to not push this command when I am working on other commands but I try to consistently speak the word with a certain action because they will eventually come to understand it as a release from what they were previously doing.

When you go to teach and reinforce this command give them one of the other commands and after you treat get them to stand up or move around and as soon as they do speak the word giving another treat. If they haven't already gotten the concept of this word doing this exercise will help reinforce that they are free to move. Always give this cue at the end of any training session and allow them to roam freely about the area you are working in to also help reinforce this command.

**Wait**- I typically teach wait when I am training my dog to walk on the leash but it is also a great command to have them wait at a door way or keep them from jumping out of your when you first open the door. This command isn't one that is always taught but it can be used in many different applications.

There are a few ways you can teach wait; you can teach it in a combination with walking or when you are teaching other commands as well as a more basic approach. I will give you some pointers in all of these areas so you can use whatever combination will work best for you and your furry family.

To use when they are on the leash wait until they are walking well then let the leash relax and give them some free reign. As they start to get ahead of you speak the wait command and see if they stop their forward movement until you catch up. If they do give them big praise and a treat. If they do not apply pressure to the leash to keep them stopped and keep applying it as you catch up with them continuing to speak the wait command and then give them a treat when you reach them. If you repeat this a few times they typically quickly pick up on, wait means if they stop moving till you catch up they get a reward. This will make them want to wait up for you because they associate it with good things. You may have to progress with holding them in the wait position the entire time you catch up and as they catch on you may only need to give light tugs to keep them in place if they go to move until you eventually can catch up without needing to give any leash cues.

When we have a well behaved dog we can take them on walks and let them roam ahead and explore. This allows them to have some more fun and gives you a break from the constant walking and once they have a good grasp of the wait command you don't have to worry about your pup getting to far ahead of you or running off if they see another dog coming along. You can open a door to your house or your car and not have to worry about containing a dog on top of whatever else you need to do. This confidence in your pup will make everything you do from day to day activities to trips that much easier and a lot less stressful.

# Chapter 5: Walking On the Leash

Let's start talking about walking on the leash now, you will want to attach the leash to your dog's collar or you can use a slip lead. Those are the simple leashes you see that have one loop at the end that you slip over your dog's head and easily adjusts to fit them and has a loop at the other end for your hand typically but not always. I am a fan of these leashes because it gives me and the dog I am walking a direct connection.

I know using a harness or another gadget that promises to help you walk your dog calmly is tempting and seems like an easy fix but when you use harnesses you tend to diffuse the contact between you and the dog and in many cases can actually encourage pulling. I know there are many leashes and harness set ups out their but in the end you don't need any of them and they can create more problems then actually help. For many pet parents they worry they will choke their furry friend when they pull on the leash and want to protect them so they thing the harness is best. Or they think they have more control with a harness then they do with a leash. This is a common misconception; you are making it even easier for your dog to pull you around because they aren't facing the consequences of the behavior. Not only are you allowing their behavior to make the decisions but you are losing that connect with your dog. It is so much easier for them to feel the tension or lack of through your arms when they are on a regular leash around the neck. Those subtle cues you can give are lost on a dog who is being walked in a harness.

Which ever leash set up you are more comfortable with, doesn't matter which you choose. Yes, I prefer the slip lead but if you are not comfortable with that set up your dog will sense that and in this instance you truly need to be the pack leader to get your dog to walk well with you. So to start, find your confidence while getting your pup on the leash and start walking. Keep your grip on the leash confident but soft. You want to have a feel so your dog knows you are there and in control but you don't want it to be too tight or you will create tension. The tension will translate to your dog and lead to, you got it, pulling.

Just start walking and most dogs will fall right into line with you if you have the confidence in yourself and you are projecting it properly to your dog. If they do begin to pull attempt to correct them immediately by giving a slight pull on the leash returning them to your side. As soon as you get them to your side release the extra tension you have placed on the line immediately. In this case the release will be their reward for listening. You can also add in the command wait as they are about the reach your side to start to reinforce this cue in their minds. You can also use the word or sound you have decided on as your correction word or sound. If they are familiar with this noise they will more likely hesitate when they hear it becoming aware that they are performing a behavior that you as the pack leader are unhappy with.

So give this a try and every time they begin to pull or walk in front of you instead of beside you, you will correct them and give the light pull back to your side with the command, if you so desire as well. Eventually they will get the picture that if they walk beside you, you won't keep pulling them back. This is a fine line because you do not want to get into a pulling battle with your dog. Once you start constantly pulling your dog will constantly pull and create a tug of war that will lead to no one wanting to take a walk.

So make sure you always keep your tugs short and too the point so you don't create this problem for yourself.

For some dogs, particularly ones that are very excitable this method might not necessarily work. One tactic I have found that works is every time they pull you bring them immediately back to your side and make them sit. At first this will be a little frustrating because literally every step or every other step you will be stopping and sitting. But it works because your dog will get just as annoyed. They will want to just get on with the walk already and once they realize they can keep walking if they don't pull, they will quickly change their tune so they don't have to keep stopping. You can apply the wait command here as well, every time you start to pull them back to you speak the command.

One common issue many dog owners run into is there dog pulling on the lease as they see another dog. The automatic response to stop your pup from reaching the other animal is to pull back on the leash and restrain them. By pulling back and adding tension you actually wind up making the problem worse. Your dog will feed right into that and use it to get themselves amped up and want to get to the other dog even more. Most owners don't realize that by pulling your dog back you are actually making it harder on yourself but don't fear their is a way to fix this little leash walking snafu.

Instead when you notice another animal pay attention to your dog's body language. When you see that they are beginning to give the other dog or animal too much attention then you can to redirect them. Use your sound or a tug on the leash, make sure the tug isn't a pulling match it should be a quick and decisive movement and the pressure should be released right away. You may also need the touch to almost snap them out of it, depending on how focused they get. You can use your hand like you would in normal circumstances or if you are still moving forward and want to have them continue to walk simple reach your foot out behind you and the side slightly to just make contact with their side. you want to aim for that point between their butt and ribcage for maximum effectiveness. This is by no means meant to be a kick this is just a touch to redirect your pup and get their attention back on you.

If you aren't quite ready to just walk though passing another dog, you can get them to sit and have them focus on you using the focus command. When they hold their focus on you treat them and give them lots of praise. If they can't seem to focus reinforce your unhappy with the behavior by continuing to get them to sit no matter how many times you have to ask and using your noise.

Eventually you will be walking your dog like a pro, walking your pup should feel like the easiest thing in the world. Remember when you are walking that you are the pack leader and show your furry friend you have the confidence and ability to lead them. Once they realize this they will be very willing to follow you and you will begin to enjoy your walks like you never have before. Don't forget to be consistent during your walks and really throughout all your training the more consistent you are the easier it will be for your dog to understand what you expect from them. With these tools and tips you should be feeling confident in your skills to handle any situation that arises as well as being confident that they will behave and you will have a relaxed and enjoyable walk.

# Chapter 6: Problem Solving

There are a few problems that many pet owners run into with their animals. I have included the two most common here as well as a game plan to help you overcome these challenges. Remember that training an animal to break a bad behavior can be more difficult and time consuming then teaching them a new one. Try to not let yourself get discouraged if you don't seem immediate results breaking bad habits can be a real struggle for certain dogs. Especially ones where they are in a very excited state of mind.

**Jumping:** The worst for many dog owners is when they invite someone over and your dog jumps up on your guest as soon as they walk through the door. Or your dog jumps on your when they are excited or wants your attention. Now for little dogs many people aren't very bothered by this behavior but if you have a big dog or your dog is only a puppy and still growing you will have a big problem on your hand if they keep jumping. Their jumping can knock someone ever especially a little person or make people who are already timid around dogs very fearful of yours.

But there are some techniques you can apply to teach your dog that jumping is bad. If you go through with this you have to be consistent, for many animals it is too confusing to allow them to jump on you but then expect them to know not to jump on other people. So keep that in mind as you move forward with your training to break this habit. Some key things to remember is try to not get angry if your pup jumps. Even negative attention will be giving them some kind of attention and this is why many of them will continue to jump even after you discipline them. Try to not yell or talk to them at all if you can help it, the most noise that should come from you is the sound you have decided to utilize when you discipline your pup.

The biggest key to success when your dog jumps is to ignore the behavior. As they jump up act as if they aren't there. You may have to give a quick noise letting them know you don't like the behavior or even give them a quick decisive push off of you. It shouldn't be harsh and your pet shouldn't go flying across the room, no matter how annoyed you get with them it's never good to get physical with them like that. It wont inspire their trust in you if anything it can make them fearful. But by stopping the behavior and reinforcing with your sound you can let them know you don't like it. If your dog is large and jumps on you from the front and it almost knocks you over you can put your knee up as they jump. Your knee creates a barrier that doesn't feel the best when they run into it and if you use your sound as you put your knee up you can reinforce this is a bad behavior.

Undesirable behaviors like this are harder to break then simply teaching a dog a new skill. This is something they have already learned and unlearning something can be more difficult. So don't get discouraged if after the first few sessions you haven't broken your dog of jumping all the time. Training where you are undoing something takes time and consistency.

Work on doing things that cause your pup to jump and consistently letting them know that it's not okay. If you can do this in a few short sessions a day consistently for a week or two you should see a dramatic improvement in their behavior. The activities that normally excite them should also become more boring for them if you are doing them many times a day. It will become more common for them and they are less likely to jump because they are bored with it.

I don't give treats when I teach dogs this skill because I don't feel I am asking them to do anything that deserves a treat. To me this is an expected behavior and your pup should just know to keep all four paws on the floor. When you do perform a something that usually causes them to jump and they don't, I do make a big fuss about it and try to reinforce that if they don't jump up to get attention that I will then bring the attention down to them.

Once they have mastered no jumping with you ask a friend over who isn't afraid of dogs and willing to work with you on the behavior. It's good to test their their control with someone new and exciting as well as give you practice controlling the behavior when you have guests over. Ask your dog to sit and stay away from the door until your guest is in the house, then release them and allow them to come over and sniff. Instruct your guest to ignore the excited jumping behavior and teach them they can lift their knee if they feel they need to. You as their pack leader need to watch their body language and attempt to correct them right before they go to jump. If you see the excitement growing and the front legs coming off the ground correct them with a touch and your sound. It will take some practice to reinforce this but their is no reason your dog should be jumping all over your guests.

**Letting Others into Your Home:** The last common problem many pet parents run into that I will talk about in this book is the battle that can sometimes ensue when you go to let someone in your house. Your dog or dogs go crazy, barking, jumping and you can't get them away from the door. Especially if someone knocks or rings the door bell. It almost feels like you have to battle your way to the door and then wrestle your animal away from it or else you feel like a lion tamer trying to keep them all away from the door so you can let the person in or try to keep them from running out.

I have seen many pets who walk wonderfully on the leash and will sit and wait politely to be fed or go right into their crate when asked but as soon as the door bell is rung or someone new tries to come in the house their owner seems to loose complete control.

New people are excited and sometimes your dog just can't contain their enthusiasm. Or they feel they need to be the first one at the door to check this new thing out and make sure that it is okay. Whatever the case if you have a problem with your pets behaving when you bring others into your home then apply these ideals to your training and you should be able to teach them that when someone knocks or rings the door bell they should go sit quietly in a certain spot until you allow them to come meet the new comer to the house.

Start by picking a spot in your home away from the door but where they can still see the door for your dog to go to. Making sure that they can see the door is important because they will still feel involved and you can also keep an eye on them while opening the door. When your dog can see you they are more likely to obey your command as opposed to when they can't see you, it becomes harder for them to stay focused. Pick a command that works for you but I like to use the word door. When I say the word door my dogs go to a certain position and wait their until I release them. This allows me the freedom to open the door and let anyone in or get a package without having to fight with dogs or worry about them running out on me.

Once you have picked your spot and your command word I want you to walk your dog to the spot and have them sit while saying the command word. Once they are sitting give them a reward. Repeat this step multiple times until your dog starts to get the hang of it. They should start to move towards to position as soon as you say the word. Once they have masters then first part you can move on to the next step.

Now add the next element after they have moved to the position and are sitting add the command to stay. This is when hand signals can come in handy because you can give the hand cue to stay and reinforce the overall cue of door by speaking it. As they stay you will begin to step away from them making it further and further just like you did when you were teaching stay then returning to them and rewarding them before giving the cue to free them. Repeat this until you can walk to the door without them moving or following.

Next start to open the door when you get to it. If your dog stands up when you open the door or moves calmly return to them and reset them in the position you asked them to stay in. Once you can open the door without movement start stepping outside every briefly. This will allow you to collect packages or maybe take out without having your dogs move because they can't see you anymore.

The next part you will add in a knock or your door bell. You can knock yourself on anything in your house and then give the command door. When you add these noises in it may be harder to get your pup to move into position. If this is the case add the noise but restart with the steps in the beginning where you first move them to the position and then eventually stay and then starting to walk over to the door. Some dogs will pick up what you want and you wont have to repeat this step with the sounds but for some dogs this can be very difficult at first.

Once they have mastered this then you can add in that awesome friend who doesn't mind helping you train your dogs. Apply the same concept as you did with adding the sound. You friend may be outside ringing your door bell or knocking for awhile before you able to open the door. Once they can see the persons outline and still sit and wait for you to open the door then you can invite them in. If you pup gets up reset them again. Make sure your guest ignores them if they come up to them and allow you to do the reinforcing. Try to remain calm and ignore the behavior while training. If you act like this is no big deal and an everyday thing they will start to treat it that way as well.

Remember to work at your dogs pace if they seem like they are struggling with the next step go back one and work on that one some more, reinforcing it again before moving on. Also remember to keep your sessions short as your dog will only pay attention for so long before they stop retaining the lesson you are trying to teach. And finally remember to repeat what you were doing in the previous step a few times before moving on to the next step. This repetition helps get your dog in the right frame of mind and can help make progressing to the next step even easier for them.

# Chapter 7: A Few More Tips

There are many methods out there to help with dog training and there are also many little tips and tricks that pet parents can use to help them along the way. I have laid out a few more tips here to help you when training your pup. Hopefully these will help answer any questions you may have from the material by giving more detail that a certain section may have held.

**Remain Calm:** Our furry friends can be frustrating and infuriating at times, chewing things, going to the bathroom in the house or knocking you over by jumping up. Whatever the case may be it can get frustrating and hard to control your temper at times. But giving into your anger is one of the worst things you can do when working with your dog. You are more likely to teach them to fear you then to get them to respect you. Do your best to remain calm in your actions as well as with your words. This really can be tough when your dog is making you nuts with their behavior but when you can remain calm and in control you are more likely to get the response from your dog that you desire.

**Treats:** To start with let's talk about treating your dog. Treats are a great tool to help you with training. There are very few animals that can't be motivated with food so don't be afraid to use them to get results. I always recommend small treats about the size of your dog's food. When you give bigger treats they can fill up faster and you don't want to make them sick by over treating. Also by measuring out a "cup" of dog treats you can adjust what you feed your dog daily to keep from over feeding them. This way they are still getting the same amount they would normally.

When you are using treats as a motivation for training make sure once they start to get the idea of training, you offer other types of rewards. Try things like playing with a special toy with them or even just lots of pets and enthusiasm. While food is a great motivator and can help get your message across to your dog, if you use it all the time you pet will come to expect it and you can wind up with a dog that will only listen when you have a treat. So make sure you don't allow the treats to become a crutch or you will hurt your training progress in the long run.

Some dogs can extremely excited about treats, when this happens they can nip you in the process of taking the treat and you risk getting bit in their excitement. First I want you to realize that if they do bite you it was most likely not their intention but that they were just so excited to get the food they didn't think about being careful. Second I want you to then help them to change the response to those treats so not only are your hands safe but anyone else who may handle the dog will be safe as well.

If you have a very excitable dog when giving treats you should teach them the command gentle. As they go to take the treat hold it in your hand in a manner that they wont be able to get it out unless you release your hand and let them. Not only will the very small amount of exposed food force them to focus more but it also gives you control so you can stop them from taking the food if they get to excited or pushy about it. When they do start to take the treat gentle say the command word gentle and then give them praise to let your pup know that was the exact behavior you were looking for. Sometimes giving the focus command before giving up the treat can help calm them and get them focused on the task at hand. You may get nibbled a little as your start this process but as long as you hold the treat in your hand and try to keep it in an almost fist you can protect your fingers from those excited moments in the beginning. But this command is worth learning if you have a dog who needs it. You may get some nips in the beginning while they are first learning but it will set them up for a lifetime of good behavior and save your fingers in the future many times over.

**Commands:** When and how you give your commands is so important. The tone of your voice and the timing you use when you are training can make or break your training in certain cases. Use these guidelines to help you find the right tone of voice as well as when to say the command or cue word while your training so that you reinforce the correct behavior.

Many people new to dog training make the common mistake of delivering the cue or command word at the wrong time. For example, if you are trying to teach your dog to come and instead of waiting till the dog is already approaching you to give the cue word. You instead give the command hoping they will simply listen to what you are asking and perform the command. When you give it to early in this situation you are actually teaching them to not come to you when you give the command. You are inadvertently reinforcing that command with not coming in their mind when you say it over and over again without them coming to you.

With that in mind, when you first start training if you wait until your pup is already approaching you before speaking the command word then they will start to associate the word with the action. The same goes for sitting, laying down, etc. You want to reinforce the action with the word after they have achieved the position or are already moving into the desired position. Eventually they will be able to perform the command when you say it but in the beginning you can't expect them to understand if you haven't taught them yet.

The tone of voice you use to give your commands is also important. If you have the wrong tone you can convey the wrong message to your dog and get undesired results. This can be difficult to control sometimes when your furry friend is being difficult or if you haven't really found your confidence yet. If your tone is too loud or too angry your dog may become scared to come or obey your command because they are fearful and unsure about your tone. If it's too soft or timid they will most likely not respect it. Your pup will take it as more of a request then a command and will more times then not refuse to perform the requested command.

You want to find a happy medium in between the two. If you can keep a calm tone to your voice while still infusing it with confidence and command, you will get a much better response from your animal. While dogs for the most part respond to body language we as humans communicate vocally. I have found that for humans when you can find that right tone of voice the proper body language your dog needs to sense to listen will automatically be conveyed.

**Hand Signals:** Hand signals can be a great tool for teaching your dog what you want from them. While dogs can be taught to understand voice cues they aren't necessary. We as humans need the vocal cues more then your pup does. Adding in a hand signal to your dogs training can help give them a visual cue to help them understand what your asking. There are a variety of cues you can use but the key to success is use a consistent cue for each signal so you don't confuse them. You add this signal in when ever you give your verbal cue. Eventually they will come to associate the hand signal with the action. Here are some of the cues that I use.

Sit- Use closed fist with closed fingers facing you and on top.

Down- point to the ground

Stay- open hand, palm facing your pup.

Focus- Pointer, thumb and middle finger come together almost as if you were going to make the okay signal but tuck your remaining two fingers down. You should have your thumb and pointer finger side of your hand facing you.

Free- With open hand and open fingers turn your palm to face the ceiling and point fingertips down slightly. As you say the command word move your hand forward and away from your body.

Wait- I use the same hand signal as stay because the concept to wait is the same you are asking them to stay in whatever spot they are currently in until you catch up or give the cue that they are free to move ahead again.

# Conclusion

I want to thank you for downloading this book and I hope I was able to give you some great tips and tricks for helping you on your journey with training your dog. Our furry friends don't really understand when we talk with them or when we really need them to do or not do something. This can be extremely frustrating especially if you aren't prepared with the right tools to train them. You can both wind up frustrated and more anxious then you were prior to trying.

My hope is with this guide and step by step directions for many useful training cues, you and your pup will become a happy and well balanced pair or pack. Just remember you need to be the pack leader to inspire your dog to want to listen to you, to work at your dogs pace and that positive reinforcement will always get you better results. If you can keep these three main concepts in mind throughout your training sessions, you will have a lot of success with your animals.

Training can be a difficult and frustrating path but I hope we have made your journey that much easier with the information we have provided here for you. If you do get frustrated take a deep breath and try again. Sometimes you may need to move back a few steps and work there for a bit before moving on again. If this happens it really is okay. Every dog and human is different and everyone's pace is different so try to not set a timeline for yourself. Just keep working and eventually you will have a happy, well trained dog who you will want to take everywhere with you.

If I was indeed able to make your journey easier I hope you will give this book a review online and and share your experience with others. Any feedback is always greatly appreciated to help to improve the content I provide and give my readers the best experience possible. Questions to problems are also welcome though I tried to cover topics many dog owners struggle with if there are other issues I didn't think of I will cover them in my next book for you. I look forward to hearing from you.

# Special Invitation!

If you liked what you read and would like to read high quality books, get free bonuses, and get notified first of **FREE EBOOKS,** then join the official Xcension Publishing Company Book Club! Membership is free, but space is limited!

You can join the Book Club by visiting the link below:

http://www.xcensionpublishing.com/book-club

# FREE Bonus!

As promised, here is your free bonus! Visit the links below to download your free 1 hour interview with professional dog trainer and dog behavior consultant, Howard Weinstein! Also included is the word for word transcription of this amazing interview!

http://www.xcensionpublishing.com/DogTraining.mp3

http://www.xcensionpublishing.com/DogTrainingBonus.pdf

37540481R00033

Made in the USA
Middletown, DE
30 November 2016